Contents

Written by
David Grant

Illustrated by
Dylan Gibson
and **Andy Stephens**

Series editor **Dee Reid**

Heinemann

Part of Pearson

Characters

Kris

Kelly

Jake

Billy Green

Tricky words

- genius
- sighed
- quietly
- explained
- database
- heard
- instead
- excluded

Read these words to the student. Help them with these words when they appear in the text.

Introduction

Kris and Jake are best mates. Kelly is in their year at school. She is a computer genius. Most of the time, Kris and Jake get on well with Kelly but sometimes they are not sure about what she is up to on her computer. One day, Kelly and Kris went round to Jake's house. Kelly was showing Kris and Jake how to hack a phone.

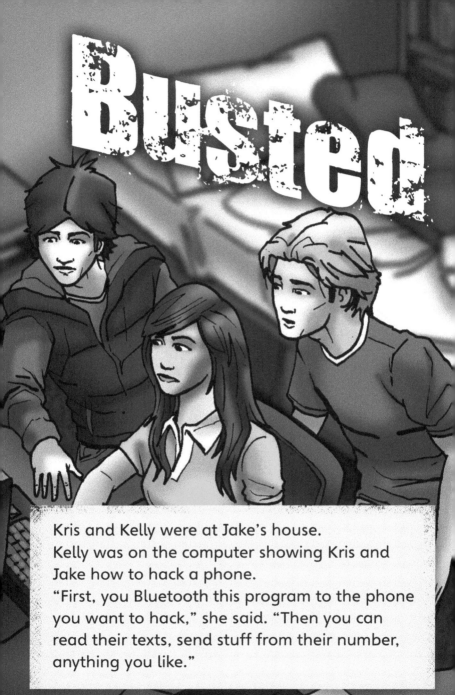

Busted

Kris and Kelly were at Jake's house.
Kelly was on the computer showing Kris and
Jake how to hack a phone.
"First, you Bluetooth this program to the phone
you want to hack," she said. "Then you can
read their texts, send stuff from their number,
anything you like."

"That's amazing!" said Kris. "Is it really that easy?"
"Only when you know how," said Kelly.
"She's genius, isn't she?" said Kris.
But Jake didn't say anything.
"What's the matter with you?" asked Kris.
"Nothing," sighed Jake.

"Something is wrong," said Kris. "You look like somebody died. What's the matter?"

"Well," said Jake quietly, "you know Billy Green and his mates? They keep texting me and emailing me stuff."

"So?" asked Kris.

"They're saying stuff about me," Jake explained.

"What kind of stuff?" asked Kris.

"Nasty stuff," said Jake.

"That's bullying," said Kelly.

"It's OK," said Jake. "I just ignore it."

"You can ignore it if you like," said Kelly, "but I'm not going to."

"What are you going to do?" asked Jake.

But Kelly was already typing on the computer.

"Hey, that's my email," said Jake, pointing to the computer screen. "How did you get in there?" Kris laughed. "Kelly can do anything on computers," he said. Kelly carried on typing.

Then, the screen changed again.
"What's that?" asked Kris.
"The school database," said Kelly.
"It's where they keep all the information about the teachers and students."

ST. STEPHENS HIGH SCHOOL

Billy Green

"Billy Green!" said Kris, pointing to the picture on the screen.
"It's not his photo we're interested in," said Kelly.
"It's his personal stuff we want."

"Who else has been bullying you?" Kelly asked.
Jake told her the names of Billy's friends.
Kelly looked them up on the school database.
She saved their email addresses on her phone.
"What are you up to?" asked Kris.
"You'll see," said Kelly. And she smiled.

At breaktime the next day, Kelly was talking to Kris and Jake.

But when she saw Billy Green and his friends, she walked over and stood near them.
Then she got her phone out.
It looked like she was texting.
Then she came back again.

"What are you doing?" asked Kris.
"Nothing," said Kelly. "Just sending
my new friends some stuff on Bluetooth."
"Why are you sending stuff to
those idiots?" said Kris.
"You'll see," said Kelly.

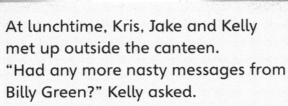

At lunchtime, Kris, Jake and Kelly
met up outside the canteen.
"Had any more nasty messages from
Billy Green?" Kelly asked.
"No," said Jake. "Not since breaktime."
"Maybe they got bored and started
picking on someone else," said Kris.
"Maybe," said Kelly. And she smiled.

The next day, Jake ran up to Kelly and Kris.
"You'll never believe it," said Jake.
"Billy Green and his mates got called
out of the lesson to go to the headteacher.
And they never came back!"
"I know," said Kelly.
She was smiling.

"You know what I heard?" said Kelly. "I heard they'd been sending nasty texts and emails to someone. But somehow all the texts and emails they sent yesterday didn't go to the person they thought they were sending them to. They went to the headteacher instead."

"You mean Billy Green and his mates have been bullying the headteacher?" said Kris. Kelly nodded.

"They've been excluded," Kelly said.
"Honest?" said Jake. He looked really pleased.
Kris began to laugh.
"You did it, didn't you Kelly?" said Kris. "You messed up their phones and their email so all the messages they sent to Jake went to the headteacher instead!"

Kelly looked surprised.
"No!" she said. "I don't even know how to do that kind of thing. I just heard that's what happened. That's all."
And she smiled.

Quiz ////////////////////

Text comprehension

Literal comprehension

p5–6 Why was Jake unhappy?

p15 How did Kelly help Jake to get back at Billy Green and his mates?

Inferential comprehension

p4 Why does Jake not want to admit he is being bullied?

p14 What do you think the headteacher thought when he got the texts and emails?

p16 Do you think Kelly was responsible for Billy Green getting excluded?

Personal response

- Have you ever been bullied by text or email?
- Do you think being excluded will stop Billy Green from bullying?

Word knowledge

p6 Which word means 'to take no notice'.

p9 Find a word made of two words.

p12 Find an adjective.

Spelling challenge

Read these words: **friend**   **heard**   **yesterday**

Now try to spell them!

Ha! Ha! Ha!

What did one keyboard say to the other keyboard?

Sorry, you're not my type!

Find out about

- How we used to send messages and how we send them today.

Tricky words

- probably
- urgent
- pigeon
- electrical

- expensive
- heavier
- ordinary
- university's

Read these words to the student. Help them with these words when they appear in the text.

Introduction

How did we send messages before we had mobile phones? Hundreds of years ago, pigeons were used to send urgent messages. Then the postal service was started and letters were carried by horse. Then telegrams were invented. These were messages sent down electrical wires using Morse code. Today we use mobiles or Facebook.

Get the Message

What do you do if you're meeting a friend but you're going to be late?

You probably send them a text message.

But what was it like before we had mobile phones?

How could you get a message to someone quickly?

Pigeon post

Hundreds of years ago, the quickest way
to send an urgent message was by pigeon.
Pigeons were used because they always
fly back to their home. Pigeons fly fast!
They can travel more than 933 miles at up
to 50 miles an hour.

The problem was that you could only send
a message to one place – the place where
the pigeon lived – and you had to remember
to take a pigeon with you if you wanted to
send a message.

The postal service

Then, in 1635, a postal service was started.
The letters were carried by horse.
The horses could travel up to 118 miles
a day, but this meant that it would take
more than a week to send a letter from
London to Edinburgh and get a reply.

Telegrams

Sending messages started to get quicker in 1845.
That's because telegrams were invented.
Telegrams were messages sent down electrical
wires using Morse code.

Morse code is a way of spelling letters
using different numbers of dots and dashes.
For example:

The letter 'A' is ·— (dot dash)

The letter 'B' is —··· (dash dot dot dot)

Morse code

A ·—	M ——	Y —·——	6 —····			
B —···	N —·	Z ——··	7 ——···			
C —·—·	O ———	Ä ·—·—	8 ———··			
D —··	P ·——·	Ö ———·	9 ————·			
E ·	Q ——·—	Ü ··——	. ·—·—·—			
F ··—·	R ·—·	Ch ————	, ——··——			
G ——·	S ···	0 —————	? ··——··			
H ····	T —	1 ·————	! —·—·——			
I ··	U ··—	2 ··———	: ———···			
J ·———	V ···—	3 ···——	" ·—··—·			
K —·—	W ·——	4 ····—	' ·————·			
L ·—··	X —··—	5 ·····	= —···—			

Telegrams were much faster than sending
a letter by horse but they were also
much more expensive.
People only used telegrams for sending urgent
messages, like 'Mother ill. Come quickly'.
In 1913, 82 million telegrams were sent in the UK.

The first telephone

Then, in 1876, Alexander Graham Bell invented the telephone and contacting people started to get much easier.
But you could only make a phone call from your home. The first public phone box wasn't built until 1921.

Mobile phones

It was another 62 years before you could buy a mobile phone.
In 1983 the world's first mobile phone went on sale. You could talk on it for an hour but then you had to charge it for 10 hours.

The first mobile phones were 30cm tall and weighed 750 grams. That's more than 5 times heavier than an iPhone!
The price was even heavier.
It cost $3995, which is around £6000 in today's money.

If you want to send a quick message to your friend today, you would probably send a text message. The first text message was sent in 1992 but texting took a long time to become popular. In 1996, most mobile phone users sent just 5 texts a year.
In 2009, some mobile phone users sent over 22,000 texts a year.

The internet

Text messages aren't the only quick way
of contacting your friends now.
You can also send them a message by
computer, using the internet.
The internet started in the 1960s.
It was used by the American army to
send information around the world.
But it was only in the 1990s when ordinary
people started using the internet.

Social networking

In 2003, social networking sites started to become really popular.
MySpace was the first really successful site like this.
In 2004, an American student called Mark Zuckerberg hacked into his university's computer network and copied pictures of the students.

He put them on a new website which he called Facemash. 450 people visited the website in its first 4 hours.

He renamed the website Facebook and by 2010, 500 million people around the world had signed up for the most popular social networking site ever.

Sending a message today is easy and quick.
We look back at homing pigeons and telegrams and we think they are slow and strange.
One day, we might look back at texting and email and think they are just as slow and strange!

Quiz ////////////////////////

Text comprehension

Literal comprehension

p20 What was not so good about using pigeons to send messages?

p26 What was not so good about early mobile phones?

Inferential comprehension

p23 Why did people only send brief messages in telegrams?

p24 Why was it important that public phone boxes were built?

p27 Why do you think it took a long time for texting to become popular?

Personal response

- Why do you think texting is so popular?
- Have you ever sent a text in an emergency?

Word knowledge

p19 Which two words are contracted in 'you're'?

p23 Find a word that means the opposite of 'cheap'.

p28 Find a word that means 'getting in touch'.

Spelling challenge

Read these words:

you're   carried   someone

Now write them from memory!

Ha! Ha! Ha!

What happens if you get a gigabyte?

It megahertz!